Collective Wisdom

Collective Wisdom
by Gregg Robinson

ALL RIGHTS RESERVED

ISBN # 978-0-578-62694-9

Distributed by Amazon

© 2019 Gregg Robinson

2nd Revision January 2025

Editing & Layout Created by Laura Reynolds

CONTENTS

- 5 — Purpose
- 7 — How to Use this Book
- 9 — Acknowledgments
- 12 — Cash in — Cash out = Surplus
- 16 — The Vehicle Drain
- 23 — The Importance of Geography
- 26 — Couple Up
- 30 — Create Your Own Families
- 34 — Dinner Club
- 44 — The 5 Grand Principle
- 50 — Usurious Credit Cards
- 68 — Financial Planning at this Stage of the Game
- 74 — Fresh Food *Is* **Cheaper** and **Healthier** than Packaged Food
- 80 — Tool Sharing
- 84 — Net Worth Wipe Out
- 96 — The Asian Playbook
- 102 — And When You Have A Plan
- 106 — The Market at this Stage of the Game
- 114 — The Subject of Insurance
- 120 — Good Credit
- 124 — A Different Overhead Reduction Strategy
- 125 — Final Thoughts
- 127 — About the Author

COLLECTIVE WISDOM

INTRODUCTION

• •

THE PURPOSE OF THE BOOK IS TO SHARE WITH YOU MANY SIMPLE TRUTHS. TO SHARE AND AFFIRM IDEAS, STORIES AND OTHER LINES OF THOUGHT ON HOW EACH AND EVERY ONE OF YOU CAN CREATE SURPLUS IN YOUR LIFE.

GREGG ROBINSON

COLLECTIVE WISDOM

Purpose

The Purpose of this book is to be that little guide, the one on the shelf not too far away, the little reinforcer. The one that reaffirms you in your beliefs. The one you can reach for when you need a pick me up or a ray of sunshine. The one that helps you achieve what you want to achieve.

Yes, this book is for people who want to do something – big or small. It doesn't matter what it is – that is for you to decide.

The book is also written from the perspective that we are all free to choose what we do with our lives. On these pages are age old wisdoms, updated for modern life at the beginning of the 21st century. A simple instruction set for creating surplus in your life.

It is through surplus, in both time and money, that ordinary human beings can do great things.

GREGG ROBINSON

COLLECTIVE WISDOM

How to Use this Book

The book is written so that you can pick and choose what works for you. Why? Because each idea for creating Surplus in your life is a stand-alone idea. You can pick one, you can pick many. But pick one and stick with it for a year.

Run the idea you chose like it's a business. Why? Because it's about the business of making your life richer – socially or financially. Many ideas are both. After you re-read the idea a few times you may see the wisdom. Or you may see it after a year of implementation. Regardless, the light will come.

The Format is simple.

Chapter Title is the concept… or about someone who embodies the concept.

The text on the same page are highlights or suggested action steps.

The Backstory gives you more understanding. Explains action steps in more detail. Provides for you a thought process to make the idea yours. The goal is for you to own it. Embrace it. Sometimes it will tell the story of why the concept is so important. Sometimes it will share something I have witnessed or observed in contemporary life. Many times, it will encourage you to take this action step and why. At all times, it is not just about money.

GREGG ROBINSON

COLLECTIVE WISDOM

Acknowledgments

• • • • • • • • • • • • • • • • • • •

This book is dedicated to my children Nina and Mekdelawit.

CASH IN − CASH OUT = SURPLUS

Want more?

→ Reduce your Expenses
OR
→ Make more Money... it's that simple

Treat yourself like a business... an entity... a being that gets things done.

Surplus goes to a purpose.

GREGG ROBINSON

Cash in — Cash out = Surplus

WAGES PER HOUR

(x 40 HOURS PER MONTH)

—

RENT, CAR, FOOD...

= SURPLUS

The truth of the matter is **getting a surplus at the end of the month is in many ways hard**. Unless you are in an industry that pays high wages or hold a college degree or two, it takes some work to get a surplus at the end of the month.

Even making more than $20.00 per hour is not a guarantee of the good life if you are fool hardy. And in truth, a college degree doesn't protect you from making poor financial decisions. Good guidance does.

What do you want for your life?

→ And here's the deal — it's all compared to how much you bring in, and what you want for your future.

> What is the definition of foolhardy?
>
> Spending too much money compared to your income on: shoes, booze, cosmetics, hair extensions, the opposite sex, the same sex, video games, or cable TV... just to name a few

COLLECTIVE WISDOM

IT DOESN'T MATTER HOW YOU START

Interestingly enough – it doesn't matter if you are making $10.00 an hour, living at home with Mom, if you are banking it all. Let's say you don't spend a dime, not real, but let's say you did. You would have close to $16,000 – 18,000 (let's not forget taxes) in the bank by the end of the year. In truth, you will be better off, if your goal is to get a nest egg together, than your buddy making $55,000 a year at his starter dream job in the big city spending every cent he makes. That starter dream job looks great on paper. Yet, if he has the super cool apartment by himself, pays for a car and has other operating expenses above the correct percentages of what he should be spending, dines out all the time because he is busting his balls on the new career... etc. etc. As you can see, he's having a good time advancing his career, yet he is not really getting ahead.

The real point is you can start anywhere... and at any time.

> **The two ways to create monetary surplus in your life are the same two ways to create other surpluses in your life.**

For the gal living at home who puts her nest egg together and gets the big job finally after working near-minimum wage for two years. Or, for the guy who blows every cent of his paycheck for the first two years and gets all the gizmos he wants and is now ready to cool his jets and be more sensible about his finances. Or, even the person who has to rebuild their financial life after a divorce or death of a spouse. No matter where you find yourself in life, you have options to get back on track. You have options to create surplus in your life.

COLLECTIVE WISDOM

THE VEHICLE DRAIN

• • • • • • • • • • • • • • •

#BICYCLE
#CARPOOL
#UBER
#OVER 25% SAY NO

#GET ONE WHEN YOU REALLY CAN AFFORD IT

GREGG ROBINSON

The Vehicle Drain

Popular culture promotes spending every dime you have. And hundreds of thousands of people are not immune... Or said differently... ***popular culture promotes making unwise or untimely decisions, sometimes.***

While a hot auto is a phenomenal piece of creativity – you have to treat it as a goal, not an end. It has been a rite of passage in our culture that once you get your first job, or reach the age of 16, you go out and get your first car. Well, what I am promoting is – *not*.

What I am suggesting is: if you don't have to, don't. Yet, why is that?

Well if you live in a big city, your operating costs per month start to get obscene... meaning: knocking out too large a chunk of your take home pay.

We know enough about monthly expenses to know that if you are spending more than 25% of your take home pay on the car note, gas, maintenance and insurance, you're spending too much money. Yes, you have to take it all into account to really get the big picture.

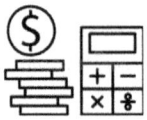

So can you really create a surplus in your life with such a large chuck coming off the top? The answer is no.

COLLECTIVE WISDOM

AUTO MATH

If you are pulling down minimum wage or not much more, the auto math just doesn't work for you. At least not for a new car.

$$10.00 \times 40 \text{ hours} = \$400.00 \text{ per week}$$

(no taxes or any other benefits taken out)

$$\times 52 \text{ weeks} = \$20,800.00 \text{ per year}$$

Now take out federal taxes

$$\begin{array}{r} \$20,800.00 \\ -2,309.00 \\ \hline 18,491.00 \end{array}$$

Now divide $18,491.00 by 12, for 12 months

$$18,491 / 12 = \$1542.00 \text{ per month} \quad \text{(your take home pay roughly without other taxes coming out)}$$

$$\$1542.00 \times 15\%$$

(all the budget books say 15 percent is a number you should pay for auto expenses including car payment, car insurance, gas, and maintenance)

Therefore:

$231.00 /month is your target number for auto expenses

For Real!

The math flat out doesn't work for many people to have a car. In a car dependent area like the one I live in, this is really bad news. But it also is not something to dwell on. It's an issue that has to be conquered. So how do you tame this beast?

#GETTING IT TOGETHER

GREGG ROBINSON

YOU'VE GOT TO FIND A NEW GROUP TO TAME THIS BEAST

When life was more cohesive, people in the same neighborhoods worked at the same places. Recreate this cohesion today. Modify your rugged individualism, a bit, and reach out to other people in your neighborhood who work where you do... ***and carpool.***

I will admit to you, carpooling has never been popular. It is a great idea, however no one really likes it. All of us have seen carpool lanes on major expressways in cities big and small around the United States that are rarely used. It doesn't work because it doesn't fit our lifestyle. Many people, perhaps most people, get up just early enough to get to work on time. Not a second earlier. So do you really think most people will get up 15 minutes earlier to go out of their way to pick up a co-worker and take them to work? If recent events is our guide, the answer is no.

So how do you make this work?

→ **Take care of his or her gas bill every week**. This money adds up. You have reduced your new friend's monthly expenses and you keep from buying a car until you are ready. It makes it a win-win for both people.

The only thing you have to do is be reliable and on time.

In areas that don't have public transportation, which by the way is the majority of the United States, this is one way to tame these uncontrolled costs. I offer it for you to consider.

→ **Bicycling to work** in almost every other part of the world is growing in popularity. Forget the health benefit, the benefit to your wallet is tremendous.

Don't wait for the bike lanes to be installed in your town or city. Know that you are doing the right thing for your wallet. Laugh-off your friends that are making fun of you. Know that you are making a solid business decision regarding your personal finances. Have the inner confidence to know you are doing what is best for you at this time.

→ If you live in a city with reasonable and reliable public transportation, **take public transportation**. I happen to live in a city region that has incredibly poor public transportation. The taxis stink here too. So what do we do? We Uber.

Uber or Lyft (or any other ride sharing opportunity that has yet to be invented) is an affordable option in most areas for getting around for work and play. Frankly, I don't know how many people even made ends meet before Uber.

A BIG OMG ON THAT ONE!

THE BACKSTORY

I was ubering a young lady and child from midtown to the far east side one morning – an Uber fare of ten dollars, so far. We then dropped the youngster off at day care and proceeded to take this young lady to work back into the center of town: another 7 dollars of fare. Assuming she had to do the same thing that evening, this woman spends $34.00 a day on transportation – and this is Uber. If this young lady earns $10.00 per hour, she spends over 40% of her total pay on transportation per day.

It's common knowledge in our town that taxis cost twice the price of Uber. Can you imagine spending $68.00 a day on transportation? I have speculated this woman makes $10.00 an hour. Even if she worked ten hours that day, if she had to have taken a taxi that day, she would have spent over 2/3 of her daily paycheck on transportation.

Positive Actions

→ Least popular would be carpooling. Government types have been hawking the benefits of carpooling for years to little avail. It's never been popular. Millions of people travel in cars by themselves and have been going to work like this for decades now. Recently introduced carpool lanes in most parts of this big nation still go pretty empty even during rush hour. It is however, one way to skin this beast. Find a friend or two with whom you work, who live near you or along the way to work and offer them carpool money. Reducing a friend's or new friend's gas expenses add up.

→ Used cars are always the way to go to reduce your monthly auto expenses. Go into a dealership with the number you want to pay per month and see what they have on the lot. Or even better, call first. Call a sales person when the showroom, new or used doesn't matter, when they are not busy and he or she will be very helpful. Mornings are good – Saturdays are not. You can find something in the low $100.00's... you have to work at it... It may not be your dream car, but it will get you to work and back. Today, the new owner of a used vehicle can also, on many makes and models, get an extended warranty for reasonable dollars. For someone starting out, the numbers really need to be examined. Meaning, you have to do the math. For a person well above minimum wage, it makes a lot more sense again only if the numbers add up.

Many used cars do have somewhat lower insurance rates. If you, your best friend, or you Dad/Mom have an established relationship with an insurance agent call them. Discuss with them which 2 or 3 vehicles you are considering buying and find out which one is the cheaper to insure. Ah-ha! If you didn't know, you know now, that the cost of replacement parts (and related factors) and labor are put into a math formula and the end result is the cost of your car insurance on an annual basis.

You have two key decisions to make: the type of vehicle you want and its cost; and what level of insurance you want for a vehicle. Replacement and rebuild costs of a damaged vehicle are set. There is nothing you can say or do to change them. The dealership or repair shop that you take your car to get repaired, once approved by your insurance company, are paid at a set rate – Period.

→ Move closer to work. Since the cost of transportation is so high now days, it really is worth considering moving closer to one's job. For many people the cost of transportation is too high, as a percentage of our take home pay. Therefore, it really makes sense for many people who are making less money to move into walking distance of your job, if you can. In truth, it makes sense for people of all income groups to live as close to their work as reasonable. Thought leaders, professionals in many fields believe our quality of life is being sucked away on our expressways. Believe as you want, but moving closer to work provides a lot of value. Or a short Uber ride.

→ Uber or Lyft (or any rideshare arrangement in your area) is a great way to eliminate auto payment and auto insurance costs. However, it only makes sense if you are a reasonable distance from work. I would love to state that this is the perfect solution for most people, however you still have to do the math. While $100.00 per week in Uber expenses makes sense if you are going to pay in excess of $600 – $700 a month in car and car insurance payments (per month), at $200.00 per week it may not. Again, do the math.

THE IMPORTANCE OF GEOGRAPHY IN CREATING SURPLUS

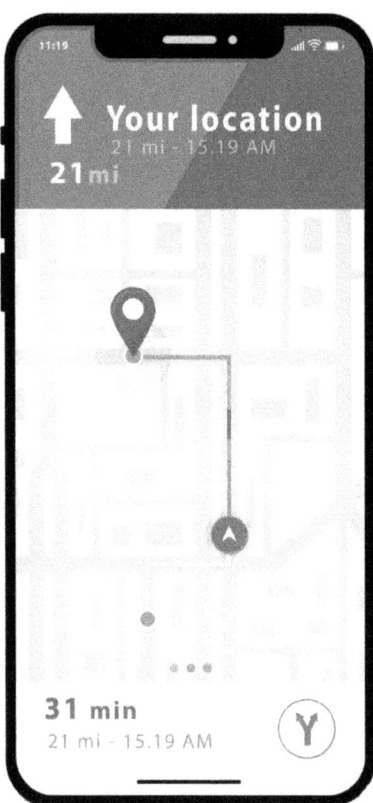

> Live as close to work as is reasonable. The savings in commuting time, the addition of more personal time for you can lead to peace of mind, more family time, or more time to accomplish other areas of interest. *It's just that simple.*

The Importance of Geography

The author lives in a city region that firmly believed that the automobile would be the answer to all of our transportation needs. It had such confidence in that vision that it ripped up all of its trolley tracks. Housing patterns developed that required vehicles for getting to and from work. Work patterns evolved for many of us that included commutes of 50 – 100 miles per day. Our city region isn't unique in this pattern of life. Large swaths of the United States are set up similarly. The real problem here is that commutes are generally unproductive: time-wasters so to speak.

Technology may solve this issue. The seeds are being laid right now in camera development, software development, and automotive design across the globe currently. However, right here, right now, your horseless carriage is stuck on the highway with the rest of the horses.

To avoid being robbed of this precious commodity, *time*, proximity to work, this will remain an important part of the equation in creating a good life for yourself and those you love and enjoy.

GREGG ROBINSON

Couple Up

Team UP!

Two live cheaper than one. It has been true for the ages and some things really don't change.

→ What it really means in a very practical ways is this: married, unmarried, coupled, good friends, just a cool roommate, perhaps someone you really don't know, but makes for a good roomie because they are quiet and neat.

Two incomes regardless of who makes how much eases the burden for all. And for many, family groupings make the difference between breaking even or creating a surplus every month.

Your view on the matter will vary. The communal and financial benefit can be very worthwhile.

So...

What makes for a bad roommate?

Someone you are romantically (yeah, I am being polite) linked with but have no intention of marrying or any other long term commitment. You are just playing them and being totally unfair. Save yourself the headache and the arguments because one of you isn't playing fair. Save the lost money too, because he or she is going to stick it to you good when it's all done.

Someone with a serious credit problem... you need to look twice at. It could work with a friend but you need to both sit down and set out on paper how this is going to be a win-win for both of you. This is also the only time you invade a friends' privacy by going online and doing a credit check on them. I would bring it to your win-win meeting: it expresses you mean business. *You want this to work for both of you.*

Friends or acquaintances with substance abuse issues also make poor roommates unless they're rock stars. But then if that was the case, you'd be applying to them to live off of their good fortune while you put your own financial life together, to be plain and simple. Anyway, avoid addicts at this point in your life. *It's your time to get it together.* You can help a friend after you get yourself set. Remember if the plane is dropping altitude fast, you put your own air mask on first, then you help your kids.

And there is a really good reason for it.

CREATE YOUR OWN
FAMILIES

GREGG ROBINSON

Create Your Own Families

Create Your Own Group that Shares Something...
or many things.

Part of this movement is coming out of the fiscal truths of the last ten years... It's been a jobless recovery until recently. Good jobs have been hard to come by in many areas of the country and lots of young people have been starting out and staying at minimum wage for much longer than they or their parents expected.

The other part of this movement is the understanding that there is a lot of junk that just sits in the garage most of the time. *Hmmmm*

→ Continuing along these lines, selectively sharing something of importance to you, whether it's your time or a tool in the garage can add up to something meaningful.

COLLECTIVE WISDOM

Sometimes we need a reason to talk with our neighbors. Well, sharing is one of them. And in some urban communities where the fabric of community has been rubbed raw, maybe this is a way to rebuild some of it.

SHARING MEALS

#DINNER CLUB

GREGG ROBINSON

Dinner Club

Out of all the ideas in the book for creating surplus in your life, this one really requires finding people that share your goals. Yet, it is also one of the most rewarding: forming a Dinner Club.

A Dinner Club works for:

- singles
- people that live near each other in towns big and small
- young people everywhere

#DINNER CLUB

COLLECTIVE WISDOM

Imagine...

Four neighboring families eat together every week, Monday through Thursday. Host family cooks. Dinner rotates. Each family takes a turn.

Using modest numbers, let's assume each family spends $100.00 per week on food. With dinner being the most expensive meal of the day, is it not too hard to imagine a 50% reduction in food spending per week?

The dollar amount will vary for your family. The impact is beyond financial.

#COMMUNITY   #SHARING
#DINNER CLUB   #YOUNG PEOPLE
#SENIORS   #SINGLES
#SINGLE PARENTS

What's Easier — 3 Kids or 1?

A Dinner Club is a good idea for single parents everywhere. Like-minded people with the common purpose of raising a child or two without the benefit of a partner can benefit from a 'food group' even more so than other categories of people.

Many parents know that it's easier to entertain two kids than one: they entertain themselves! Proximity to other families like yours is key. Work schedules and kids' schedules are all obstacles to getting this off the ground for singles with kids. But, if you can make it work for 2, 3 or even 4 families, it's worth the slight increase in transportation costs. In truth, the cost savings for this kind of arrangement are equal to a group of childless singles. It does require more meal coordination: simply because kids are involved. *(Grown-ups can suffer through something they don't like. Now kids... Ha!!!)* Unless everyone likes a good pasta dish, lentils over rice, a good salad... I think you get my point...the group has to like quality items that are cheap in bulk, yet tasty. After you start seeing a reduction in your operating expenses month after month, you might even splurge a bit.

#Single Parents

COLLECTIVE WISDOM

Seniors and Food

You don't have to dig too deep to learn that many seniors are mal-nourished, not because they don't have money to feed themselves, but because they lack the desire to prepare food — just for themselves. What if seniors in their own neighborhoods, in walking distance of each other or in short drives, grouped together of their own accord and took turns cooking for each other? Can you imagine how rewarding this could be! They would have company many nights a week.

Imagine a reason to do it, a few more souls to care about and nourish, and something to look forward to regularly.

This might require some coaching, yet share this with your Granddad or Mom and add to their joy of life. Remember we may all be in that position one day.

GREGG ROBINSON

City People and Sharing

Cities in movies are sometimes portrayed as big uncaring places where neighbors don't speak to each other, and sometimes worse. Well in truth, only a few neighborhoods might be like that. Over time, neighbors even in the largest of cities become real neighbors.

Now knocking on the door of your new neighbor and asking if he or she wants to be a part of your Dinner Club might be a stretch. However, one of the purposes of this book is to provide you a means to engage a neighbor over time.

Let's suppose 5 singles, again in short distances of each other, walking preferred, each cook a meal one night a week. For simplicity, the rotation is always set – the super-go-getter in the group cooks on the night he/she won't be late. Your food bill per week is cut by more than half per week, you have the camaraderie of friends, and serious dishes to wash only one night a week. *This is money in the bank.*

Who knows, you might even improve your cooking to impress your dinner friends!

Imagine: not having to do everything, every day.

COLLECTIVE WISDOM

Expand Your Nuclear Family

The nuclear family can be a trap as we move past our prime years, causing us far more expense than necessary.

→ Neighborhoods many times age together. Have you ever noticed that in some neighborhoods, all the families are old? The children have moved away... sometimes they are 30 minutes away. Often times they are in another part of the country. We live in neighborhoods of people who either look like us, think like us, or are at the same economic strata as us. Often times financially, the "are" have become a "were".

> "What do you think your older friends should do?"

I have only witnessed one out of four older relatives experience the prolonged trek of a slow deterioration to an old age where they are no longer able to take care of themselves. Two things I remember the most: the prepackaged meals from a large food chain and the overwhelming stack of medical bills. I wonder about the stubbornness this individual demonstrated to remain independent as the last remaining member of their nuclear family. I wonder about the additional stress she applied to herself in this drive to remain independent. I wonder about how the lack of nutritious food contributed to her medical conditions. I wonder about all of those home nursing visits just being company.

#GETTING IT TOGETHER

GREGG ROBINSON

Young People Everywhere

Young people everywhere can make this idea work: with the very tangible benefits of reducing their food bills per week. Food is one of those expenses that is very hard to reduce. Talk show hosts, book authors and food columnists have advised people for years on how to stretch a dollar shopping for deals in food. Yet we all know that young people, singles, and seniors really get very little benefit out of going to the big box store ten miles away and buying ten single pounds of ground chuck (for a dollar less per pound than the store around the corner), 24 rolls of paper towels, and a 3 month supply of frozen vegetables. While the dozen pack of paper towels makes sense, (and throw in the toilet tissue and the dozen boxes of Kleenex while you are at it) between food boredom and freezer burn, it rarely makes sense with someone with limited refrigeration or storage space to buy that much – at one time.

Despite the fact that in one of my favorite feel-good movies, the young female lead in an opening scene is shopping with coupons at her local grocer, I can't say I see a lot coupons being used by young people. Maybe it's popular in another part of the country: I just don't see it in my travels and this author shops fresh a few times a week. And unless you were raised and taught by a parent who can split a wooden nickel, I seriously doubt you are going to pick up the habit in your 20's. So I am not even going to suggest it. This book is about things you can really do. And with just a little bit of regularity, you can.

So I submit to you, the reader, that bulk shopping, despite its merits and potential cost savings, does little for young people, singles, and seniors. Yet even that can be tackled. One alternative is to form a buying group. This would be a smart offshoot of a

Dinner Club that really gets along and has established a layer of mutual trust. A group that knows each other well and knows each other's taste: this empowers the person delegated with the task of buying to scoop up a bargain that may not be on that week's buy list. The buyer, knowing the groups taste, can scoop up the bargain confident that he has made a good decision.

So, maybe after your Dinner Club has been around a year...!

SO WHAT'S THE REAL DEAL HERE?

The true benefit is community: sharing, raising, and benefiting from the positive interaction of adults and children. Maybe your kid can help one of the younger ones with their homework while you have some adult conversation with someone other than a work mate.

Sometimes it is hard to find people that share goals that are similar to yours. Perhaps you can try this idea out at your place of worship or your neighborhood school. Any large grouping will do.

There is power in embracing your neighbors and your neighborhood.

DINNER CLUB - A DEFINITION

A Dinner Club is the deliberate effort of a small group of families or singles to meet for dinner. Each family cooks for the group one day a week. Optimum size of the group would be four or five family units thus covering the work week. The purpose of each group is to provide its members companionship and surplus.

#DINNER CLUB

#COMMUNITY

GREGG ROBINSON

COLLECTIVE WISDOM

THE 5 GRAND PRINCIPLE

#GO SOLID #5 GRAND

#DON'T LEAVE HOME TOO SOON

GREGG ROBINSON

The 5 Grand Principle

Or, Don't Leave Home too Soon

I have talked with countless young people over the last few years and most kids are still in a hurry to leave home. Young men in particular, if not college bound, are ready to jump out of their parents' house, or often times, Mom's place, to set up shop somewhere else and live the single life. They revel in the idea of having their own crib, the ride, and the babes. I'm not mad at 'em... but fellas and ladies, because some of you in the fairer sex have parallel ideas.... *Slow down a bit*.

Here's the deal: more often than not many of you have no idea what you are getting into. And once you leave the nest, its hard coming back home. *You've changed.*

So let's give you and your Mom or Dad a number. And here it is: $5000.00 **in the bank** before you strike it out on you own.

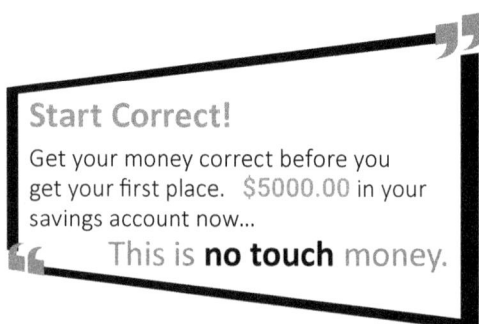

Start Correct!
Get your money correct before you get your first place. $5000.00 in your savings account now...
This is **no touch** money.

WHY? BECAUSE YOU WILL WANT FOR NOTHING.

→ $5000.00 is larger than any rent deposit you will ever make. $5000.00 is larger than any mortgage payment you will ever make. It's larger than any monthly water bill, gas bill, electric bill or cable bill that you will ever encounter as a young person starting out.

Do you see where I am heading with this? As long as you leave the house with 5 grand in the bank and a decent hourly wage, there isn't a mistake you can make on your first real job that you can't recover from. It will give you the confidence to do well, to make decisions with pride, and to give the job a little push-back if you need to so that you don't get stepped on as a newbie on the J O B.

Confidence and a solid bank account allows you the peace of mind to make good decisions.

The purpose of this section is to prepare you to start right.

THE LION'S DEN ROMAN NUMERAL ONE
Without money in the bank, you are being fed to the sharks before you even get started.

So, let's talk about that first sentence. What is going to happen if you don't start correctly and you get into trouble financially? Frankly, it's really easy if you are cutting it too close every month. The usual way this goes down is that you skip a payment on one of your credit cards. Then you get away with it for a month and you are not in the clear yet, so then you do it again. By the time the next monthly payment is due, the principle on the account has gone up a lot. So now the monthly payment is 50% more than what it was when you started skipping payments. You are out of control on this one, and your Mom says she needs $187.00 to pay her last month's cable bill. Since she thinks you are doing really well and can afford it, you give it to her. Wow, aren't you a good kid? You are, but you're going in the hole fast.

So wow, what doesn't get paid now? Ok, I got to pay the rent, but something else has to give. And holy moly *(you know what I was really going to say)* you remember that you are only scheduled to work four days next week instead of five. You go into work the next day and ask for more hours and fortunately you get them, but that just keeps you even. Can you get some overtime? The answer comes back no. So, you decide to skip the cell phone bill this month, knowing full well you can't do that twice in a row. Then up pops an oil change that you weren't planning on: 60 bucks out the door. And so you are going nip and tuck like this for 3 or 4 weeks and you whine about it so much at work, one of your co-workers suggest you go get a "pay your life away" loan. Bingo – you are had.

Sound like it can happen to you? It can happen to many of us, millions of us, only the numbers change.

So if you have taken the time to read this book, or listen to this section, take action. The $5000.00 rule can be implemented at any time. It's best to do it before you leave home. Why? Because the money and your good habits reward you over time. However, you can start in the middle of a financial problem. **You can start anytime.**

COLLECTIVE WISDOM

What if it's already started raining and it feels like all hell is about to break loose?

Positive Actions

If you are in the middle of a financial problem, stay calm and get to work. If you are hourly somewhere, the quickest and best solution is to ask for overtime. If you are salaried or hourly and you can't get more work at your current employer, the world today is full of part-time work that you don't have to go through human resources to get.

→ **Got a four-door car?** Do Uber or Lyft. Like to shop? Become a shopper for one of the shopping apps. I hear busy people, Moms in particular, tip well. Why? Because they know and value how much time you saved them. Dog-sitting, baby-sitting, house-sitting, grass-cutting, etc. are all things you can pick up in a short period of time depending on where you live, the time of year, etc.

> Got a four-door car? Do Uber or Lyft.

> Like to shop? Become a shopper for one of the shopping apps.

And here are some pointers on getting jobs lined up before you get into trouble.

→ **On your way home from work** – and this works if you live in the suburbs, the city, or the country – check out the manufacturing plant, the packaging plant, the distribution warehouse, the grocers... any place the hires more than 20 people, and put in an application. Applications usually are kept open for six months, sometimes more. If you make it through the initial sort, (now days these are digital filters performed by software – human resource people are just like anyone else) they want to work as easily as possible. If you get a call or a text, take the interview even if you are not planning on leaving your current work. If they like you, they will remember you and when you need them, give them a call.

Here in 2019, reliable people are reliable people. If they sense you are a good person, you will get a call.

COLLECTIVE WISDOM

USURIOUS CREDIT CARDS

• • • • • • • • • • • • • • • • •

GREGG ROBINSON

Usurious Credit Cards

If you find yourself in a desperate situation and have to take a credit card at a 20% interest rate or more, swallow your pride and make a promise to yourself to double down on the payments.

OK, never heard of usury? **Check your dictionary.** Unfortunately, it is time for this word to return to the popular lexicon.

Positive Actions

USURY: An interest rate above 10% in some states is considered USURY.

Double Down = make payments twice the minimum payment.

In other states not. What you need to know is that if you only pay the interest rate and never the principle, you will be paying this bill for the rest of your life. Said differently, you will never pay it off.

An exaggeration yes, but not by much.

→ Usury used to be against the law. Interest rates above 20% took a MAJOR up-tick after this most recent financial collapse. Don't ask me how this happened. And when it's all said and done, while it matters, you matter MORE! The tool for getting rid of a usurious credit card is *get rid of it.*

COLLECTIVE WISDOM

So you are at the car repair shop and "the guy" says $1,125 to get your car repaired. You don't have that much in your checking account and you don't want to touch your savings account – or you just started reading this book and you don't have it all together yet. So you do the only rational choice – you get the credit card – 'cause you need your car to get to work.

So you read the fine print… these days federal law makes the retailer or his financial agent print the annual interest rate in bold and it says 26.25 %… and you say *holy crap*. And you sign the sheet anyway. What do you do now?

What you do is double down!

This is a bill you have got to get rid of immediately. So let's say this bill starts at $25.60 per month. You pay $51.20. Double Down.

Why? Because you need to get the principle down on this bill as soon as humanly possible.

Why? Because the longer this bill stays high the larger it will grow.

Why? Because bills that charge compound interest above the rate of usury will really get out of control if you don't pay off at least the minimum every month, and on time. That means, if you are smart, before the due date.

Why? If you took algebra you can figure it out yourself. But the bottom line is this: the unpaid interest. If you don't pay your bill by the due date, unpaid interest gets added to the loan principle.

And watch out, almost all consumer loans and credit cards charge late fees for not paying your bill on time. So what happens with that fee? It gets added to your next month bill. Be very clear: it gets added to your principle.

Why? Because that's the way it works. You are paying them for the use of their money. Banks and money lenders have been with us since the dawn of civilization: check your Bible.

The goal here is to teach you how to work your money. Some banks have been real shabby lately. Some banks work in the better interest of the consumer. What I am telling you is: shop around.

Sometimes you don't have the choice. Double Down is a strategy for dealing with a bad situation.

Double pay down any bill that charges an annual interest rate above 10%. Hope it doesn't happen to you, but it has happened to lots of us. So work with it!

#USURY   #DOUBLE DOWN

TIRES AND JUDGE "J"

I was sitting in the waiting room of a tire store one afternoon watching television. I had nothing else better to do as I waited for some new tires to be installed on my car. It's rare that I watch afternoon television, so I checked it out. The judge shows were on — who stiffed who, for how much, and wow, they wanted to talk about it on television! Too funny, but I guess somebody's got to do it.

Anyway, Judge "J" comes on and one of the cases is so worth re-telling in this book: Three young ladies come on the stand; they are the defendants. What are they guilty of ...? You guessed it — non-payment of rent! The story is short and sad, just long enough for TV. However, the most striking thing in this whole episode is that Judge "J", in addition to sharing some basics about contract law, began to give these 3 young people some financial basics as well. She, however, after giving one really solid piece of advice, cut herself off, for reasons none of us will ever know. I applauded her privately because that's what these young people needed, solid advice.

What did Judge "J" say? A person should always have six months' worth of salary in your savings account. Wow, when was the last time you heard that? Have you ever heard that?

And what's the logic behind that? It is in case you ever loose your job, you will have enough money to live on until you find another one.

It's solid advice.

The young ladies on the program were not even at ground zero of basic financial understanding. They signed a contract, an apartment lease, and thought they didn't have to be responsible for its financial obligation. Wrong.

The real point here is, for my readers, builders and re-builders of their financial life, 5 grand **in the bank is a good start.**

#5 GRAND   #60 SOLID

THE PERPETUAL SLAVERY OF
INDEBTEDNESS

Wow, that's harsh.

GREGG ROBINSON

The Perpetual Slavery Of Indebtedness

Per Random House Webster's College Dictionary c. 2001, one definition of slavery is (there are many) - a state of subjection like that of a slave.

→ Usury is the practice of lending money at an exorbitant interest rate.

Usury and slavery are not mentioned, usually, in the same sentence. But I am going to offer it as food for thought.

Food for Thought

There are countless stories (and I do mean millions of young people starting out) of being offered credit cards relentlessly, in the mail. We all know someone this has happened to: it may have been you! Most likely it was. More than likely many of your friends too. While this may be good marketing, effective reach so to speak, one has to wonder about it. However, the real issue here is the interest rate being offered in those mailings.

Many, perhaps most, young people view these credit card offers as easy money. And way too many get caught in this trap early… way too early. Unless someone has schooled you in the pitfalls of credit card debt, you may be tempted to take one or two… or 6 or 7!!! Aren't you impressed when you are out shopping with a friend and she pulls out her wallet to pay, and wow – look at all those credit cards she has?

Is that friend juggling all that credit well? Or are they getting themselves into a spiral of perpetual debt? It's none of your business what a friend does with their money, or lack thereof. However, if they ask…

Not only is the volume of credit you have a problem, but again it's the interest rate you are offered at a young age that will really get you into trouble fast.

Let's face one important fact. A fact that you cannot change. Young people starting out, generally speaking, are less credit worthy than a middle-aged adult with assets. So, unless you have assets in the bank, you – young person starting out – are going to be offered a higher interest rate than your middle-aged counterpart. But the purpose of this quick story is to state not that much higher.

So why do I mention usury?

In recent years, unsolicited consumer credit offers are in excess of 20%, many times 25%. While this is no scientific study, the author has made an assumption that I live in an average area of the United States and that after chronicling unsolicited credit offers for the last seven years, I have received a representative sample.

Usury, a term in which few people even know what it means anymore, is back with a vengeance. And it's omnipresent. The term is found in the Bible and it has been with us on and off for eons. It simply is exactly as stated above: charging too high an interest rate for money borrowed.

Every state has a different percentage definition for usury. Volumes of legal work have been written on the subject with the only common agreement that usury is believed to be the practice of charging an unreasonable amount of money, as interest, for borrowed money. And that is it, my friends.

Exercise your choice and avoid high interest rates like the plague.

→ This book is going to call an interest rate of 15% and above, usury. The author will even suggest that the low teens is even usury, but the purpose of this quick story is not to start a debate. It is to offer solid financial advice. Few of us, and even fewer modern bankers are going to agree on what this number really should be. That said, I think that the majority of us will agree, that one missed or late payment should not encumber a borrower with so much additional principle so as to make it nearly impossible to pay off his or her debt in a reasonable period of time.

Wow, was that a little obtuse! *Hmmmm...* let me state my point more directly.

Compound interest should not be so high so as to make it nearly impossible to pay off one's debt in a reasonable period of time.

Scholars, TV pundits, and other informed sources can argue this back and forth until the cows come home *(another really old expression)*. Yet anecdote after anecdote, story after story of this young person and that young person caught under a mountain of credit card debt and not executing a successful strategy to get out of it, abound.

So, I offer to you, the reader, a question...isn't this a new drudgery?

Positive Actions

Avoid unsolicited credit cards and credit lines like the plague.

Get a credit card when it makes financial sense for you and at a reasonable interest rate.

Say hello to your local banker, commercial bank or credit union, and tell him or her what you are doing with your financial life and let them help. Bankers, many of those associates starting their careers behind the counter have finance degrees, can be very

COLLECTIVE WISDOM

helpful with planning, saving, and of course promoting their banks products. It doesn't hurt to listen.

And don't be afraid to go when you are already in trouble. Mind you it is better to say hello before you get into trouble, but again don't be afraid to talk. If you haven't got yourself into too deep a hole, there may be a lower interest rate that you can swap out. Banks like predictable receivables. Shop around, someone may help. Friendly, helpful people are everywhere. Sometimes you just have to find them, if you don't want to talk with your Mom or Dad.

#USURY   #GO SOLID   #GETTING IT TOGETHER

What if you are in too much Credit Card Debt Already?

Positive Actions

Pick one credit card or credit line to pay off. It makes more sense to pick the one with the lowest balance. However, you can also pick the one with the highest annual interest rate. Whichever one is going to give you the biggest sense of accomplishment is the way to go. Feel good about your decision.

Pay early – meaning before the due date. This also works to improve your credit score.

Make double payments. Get the principle down as quickly as possible.

Get a part time job. Use the money to get rid of debt, only.

#GETTING IT TOGETHER

I AM IN TROUBLE ALREADY

The Lion's Den roman numeral 2

To parents reading this book:

I can not emphasize enough that you are setting up your children to be preyed upon, like sheep, if you don't get them to have money in the bank before they leave home. $5000.00 is recommended...and a decent job of their choosing!

For parents: This is a way to have a conversation with your child and ask if they are really ready to go.

For the son or daughter: have you demonstrated to your Mom or Dad that you are really ready to leave the nest?

→ A couple of very famous comediennes of the late 20th Century have made fortunes off of incredibly funny skits about children that never seem to pack up their bags and leave home. These skits were hysterical. Whether the skit talked about continually hitting up Dad for lunch money, or how the kids don't know how to cook any food, or their expectation that the parents still do their laundry – the jokes left me rolling in the aisle. However, there may be an undertone here: maybe you haven't adequately prepared your children to leave the nest!

While you can, laugh, and sympathize with rich children who don't want to leave home because it's too damn good. I get it, who wants to be middle class and fend for yourself, when you can pretend you're rich and remain a child forever!

Most of us don't have this option. Let's not go off into this ditch.

→ Point is however, have you prepared your child to live on their own?

COLLECTIVE WISDOM

THE BACKSTORY

Around the age of thirteen, my mother pulled out the mortgage for our house. The house they built from the foundation up. She started with the amount borrowed. She showed me the interest rate. She showed me the 30-year mortgage schedule. She emphasized how the bank gets their money back first and how the loan principle is addressed at the back end of the loan. My last house mortgage frankly wasn't very different. The amount of money borrowed was a lot more. The interest rate was higher. The format and calculations were similar. The way I paid the bank back first was the same.

So, may I ask, have you shared your finances with your children? Do they know how to get it done? And, by the way, can your son boil an egg? What about potato salad?

GREGG ROBINS

COLLECTIVE WISDOM

LET'S SET SOME NEW STANDARDS

Let's Set Some New Standards

Too many young people move out of Mom's or Dad's house too early. Many don't have clear goals and too few have any money in the bank.

NOW BACK TO THE FAMOUS LADY...

I was sitting in the tire store waiting for my vehicle to be serviced and I was watching TV. It's rare I see daytime TV and I think I had already exhausted every magazine I wanted to read. That said, I am watching a very famous lady judge and she is admonishing three young ladies from the bench. Why is she admonishing them? Well because the 3 young women were in court for failing to pay rent and their excuse was they didn't have jobs. The judge informed these young ladies that they should always maintain six months of reserve in the bank just in case they ever lose their jobs. And then she stopped herself.

I don't know why. But I am going to speculate that she knew the whole concept was foreign to these young ladies. She probably also knew that on this matter it was too late to advise them. From the bench and even on TV, the only thing she could do was dispense the law as written. She may have even been saying to herself 'who let these children down by not telling them the financial facts of life'. I think her heart was showing.

So let's set a new standard: $5,000 in the bank. Period.

COLLECTIVE WISDOM

THE BACKSTORY

So why 5 grand?

Well let's look at it. For most people a few grand in the bank will get them out of anything as long as they are not unemployed too long. Think about it... your electric bill is never that large, your gas bill, your cable bill... an unexpected car problem is rarely over a thousand dollars. The usual problems caused by temporary unemployment can all be cured if you have enough money in the bank.

On the flip side... credit is even easier to obtain and maintain if the bank notices a pattern of always keeping 5 grand free and clear in one of its accounts. While I am not going to say I know the secrets of maintaining a higher credit score, clearly the factor of savings in the bank, regular deposits made into the bank, and no delinquent payments to creditors... all contribute to a healthy credit score and your overall credit worthiness.

But think about it... do you really need to concern yourself with your credit score if you always maintain 5 grand in the bank? Get real.

So for parents, tell your kids "don't leave home until you got $5,000 bucks in the bank. When you got that... I will gladly help you move out".

And kids, tell your folks "I am leaving after the first 5 grand is in the bank... not before".

FINANCIAL PLANNING
AT THIS STAGE OF THE GAME

#401K
#GO SOLID
#FUTURE GOALS

GREGG ROBINSON

Financial Planning at this Stage of the Game

Some financial planning commercials are so full of it. Saving your way to peace and tranquility and then on to some deserted isle in the South Pacific. *Oh give me a break.*

Now don't get me wrong, I am a solid believer in the promise of a secure future, but let's get a reality check on the BS. Right now, the purpose of saving for retirement for most people is so that you have enough money to maintain your lifestyle after retirement and not be a burden on your children. Many people honestly worry about having to work at McDonalds after they are forced out of higher paying jobs to make room for younger people trying to go up the ladder of success. It's a legitimate concern.

→ So the immediate advise is join your company sponsored 401K plan as soon as it is offered.

If your employer offers a 401K plan or equivalent in the public sector, fund it with a percentage of your salary to the maximum allowed. Monitor to insure you have prudent money managers at the helm of your group fund at all times.

So what's my other point? **If you got a gig that offers a savings option: take it.** If you got a gig that's hourly and not offering you any future planning help, read more and listen more to what we have to say and see if it clicks with you.

MR. AUSTIN

I was first introduced to the concept of 'directing monthly surplus' by my family barber. I owe Mr. Austin a lot of credit. Not only did he give me a great haircut once a month, he didn't pull any punches about sharing the wisdoms of his advanced age with a captive audience. After all, I was in his chair. He took full advantage, and shared. Thank you, Mr. Austin.

> Solid advice comes from many places.

Mr. Austin lived in the same small town as I did. As a matter of fact, he lived next door. He taught me about surplus. I really didn't know what he was talking about at first. I hadn't made any money out in the neighborhood cutting grass or up on the main street because my parents had more than enough work for me to do around our house. And they didn't pay. Yet, I listened and began to understand.

WHAT'S YOUR PLAN FOR RETIREMENT?

He told me you always put money away every month. I don't recall him ever saying a percentage or an exact amount. He just said "so that you have something to live on when you get old".

This particular wisdom was repeated often.

GREGG ROBINSON

PEOPLE WHO DON'T HAVE A SPARE NICKEL

People who don't have a surplus at the end of the month are nice people whose budgets are so tight, they can't see straight. Their vision clears up when they know they are not going to fall into a black hole.

Be Nice to People who Don't Have a Spare Nickel.
Find them extra work that pays.

#BE HELPFUL TO OTHERS   #CARE
#DEMONSTRATE LOVE   #TALK IS CHEAP

However, if you are just starting out...

DO MODERATE OR HIGH GROWTH OPTIONS IF YOU ARE MORE COMFORTABLE

INVEST. If you are just starting out in the work world and your employer offers you 401K benefits, take them. Oh, you don't know how it works. *Hmmm...* take them anyway. All you need to know is that the 401K is going to invest your money and that your take home pay is going to drop by 3-7% per month. (Some employees offer to match your contribution up to a certain percentage.) As long as you know that is going to happen, you are golden. It is worth it in the long run.

Now that you have done that, you can learn your job more and when you are home at night chillin', you can start reading up on 401K's and how they work at your leisure. The Internet is full of information on how 401K plans and their equivalents in the public sector work. Most investment houses are trustworthy. The company you work for hires investment managers, directly or contractually, to invest the company's money and their employees' money, so there is usually a lot of accountability here. Believe me, someone is watching the money.

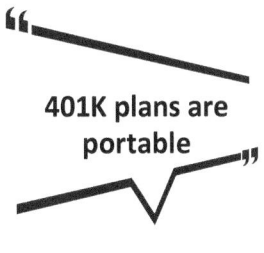

"401K plans are portable"

Almost all 401K plans are portable. Meaning you can take it with you when you leave that company. It's yours. You can take the whole amount and put it into your new company's 401K plan and keep growing your money. There are a lot more options. As you read and discuss more with your co-workers, you will learn more. This quick story is to give you the comfort level to move forward. If you have a decent paying job starting out, take advantage of a 401K option immediately. You can learn more about them as time goes on.

Go conservative on your investment choices if you really don't know jack. Then go read. Unlike medical benefits, you can change your investment choices at any time. The Internet is a beautiful thing.

If you are rebuilding your life...

If you are rebuilding your life after a financial storm like divorce or death of a loved one, just get over the storm. After the storm subsides, then start re-investing in your financial health long term. Once you get back to positive cash flow again, start re-deploying where your monthly surplus should go. The 401k or equivalent is one of those places.

> **If your employer offers 401K benefits take them**

Simple IRA plans are great for the self-employed and employees of smaller companies.

FRESH FOOD
is cheaper and healthier than
PACKAGED FOOD

Have We Talked About Fresh Food Enough?

- Fresh food is cheaper if you shop wisely and often
- Can you Cook?
- Reduce the amount of pre-packaged food and carry-out
- Fresh Food Rarely Comes in Containers for One

Fresh Food *Is* **Cheaper** *and* **Healthier** than Packaged Food

Generally speaking, this is true. You can argue this point, bring in all the experts, discuss package sizes, nutritional value etc., etc., etc., till you are blue in the face. I don't care if the super market chain that starts with an "A" has great frozen food, good quantity packs, or bargains on your favorite cracker on certain days… it flat out doesn't matter. Fresh food beats all.

However, one thing can interfere with this goal: the cost of transportation. If you don't have relatively easy access to good food outlets — meaning fresh food in your regular path of travel, e.g. to and from work. Then, unfortunately, you really have to work to get this kind of access. Funny, even liquor stores and other convenience store carry bananas now, maybe even some apples. But they don't carry enough of anything fresh to make a good meal.

For many readers this means a real change of habit. What I am talking about does require a bit of planning. Yet, you wouldn't be reading this book if you didn't want to consider making a change or two.

Buying fresh meat at a meat counter is a wonderful experience. You pick the size, you pick the cut, you decide how much you are going to spend. **You are in control.** Do you get that level of comfort when you buy frozen, breaded wing dings?

Fresh Food is Cheaper

Have you ever noticed that almost everything that is processed costs a minimum of $4.00? Plus or minus 25 cents but lets not quibble. I would really bet closer to 5 dollars, but I am playing it safe for the naysayers. This is not throwing shade on cereal manufacturers, pre-packaged meat processors, frozen pizza or any other processed food. After all, a few well-known cereals started out as health food. (They also had a lot less sugar per ounce, back then.) What this really reflects is the reality of putting food together in easy-to-package, simple-to-stack, and cheap-to-transport containers. It's the economics of moving food and getting it to you, the customer.

> **But only if you know how to cook.**
>
> **Maybe this option for creating surplus is not for you. But if it is,** work it.

Now if reducing cost in this area is a part of your plan for creating more surplus, then a reduction in packaged foods has to be a part of your action plan.

This strategy works really well with a Dinner Club.

And to be frank, this strategy only makes sense if you have four or more people to feed in your immediate family or created family. The Dinner Club strategy is a strong strategy for a group. On the flip, singles who eat out 5 or 6 days a week will also find this strategy effective. There will be a dramatic difference in retained revenue for those that can make the radical switch to preparing your own meals 5-7 days per week. Yet I have to wonder out loud if a single person can make such a significant switch in life style. That said, when there's the will there is the way.

> **Technology may solve some of this challenge.**
> Delivery of packaged essentials by the new, nationwide services are promising. However we are a few years into these services and there seems to be a consensus that no one can pick fresh fruits and vegetables better than you, the customer. We will see how this evolves.

Eating out all of the time is a significant expense for people that do that. And mind you, carry out just got more expensive with the new technology based delivery services. So don't think that you saved any money by not getting the food yourself from your current favorite restaurant. You did save time though and many times that's a good thing.

The other key piece is learning how to buy and prepare fresh food appropriate to the number of people you are caring for. Using fresh food effectively is a learned craft. If your parents didn't teach you, you have to teach yourself. Buying a whole bunch of fresh food, unless you really know or wish to teach yourself to use fresh food efficiently, is a waste of money. If you are new to this, go slow: one meal at a time.

> **Fresh food is cheaper if you know how to cook.**
> **You can teach yourself to cook.**

On the plus side, good cooks everywhere love to share. This is one area of the world that you don't ever have to pay for the information. Don't know how to do something? Ask a co-worker at lunch. If you say it loud enough someone three tables away that you don't even know will tell you everything you need to know. Perhaps an exaggeration, but not by much. Good cooks love to share.

More fresh greens, vegetables, meat and fish are better for you and can be significantly cheaper per month. But the math has to work for you.

COLLECTIVE WISDOM

WASTE

Waste, or said differently, is food you throw out because it spoiled – because you didn't have time to cook it that night or the night before or the night before that. I get it. You had to work late –yet it doesn't add up in your favor. And to add insult to injury, I bet you had one of your kids pick up carryout that night. Register a big YUCK on this one. You lost on two counts because 1) you wasted money on spoiled food and 2) you had to buy dinner out that night.

How do you handle this? How do you keep it from happening again?

Positive Actions:

ANTICIPATE. Always have one home cooked meal in the freezer or maybe two. Home cooked or heaven forbid frozen pizza, or even your favorite canned soup in the cabinet is better than carryout for maintaining the food plan for the week. Trying to get everyone in your family to agree on canned soup is probably a stretch, so pizza is the better bet. LOL. Figure it out for your family or the group of friends you call your family. Whatever you come up – it's all good. Stick to your plan and avoid last minute carryout.

And...just a thought

For a family, creating surplus is all hands-on-deck. The MVP is the second person that knows how to do everything.

Have one home cooked meal in the freezer, or two.

EVEN SPOILED KIDS KNOW HOW TO MICROWAVE, DON'T THEY!

AVOID LAST MINUTE CARRYOUT NO MATTER WHAT IT TAKES.

TOOL SHARING

#ONE LESS BILL PER MONTH ADDS UP

#USELESS STUFF IN YOUR HOUSE

GREGG ROBINSON

Tool Sharing

> These are not the most friendly of times for people of lesser means. Look at the annual interest percentage.

So its not only your garage that has a lot of things that you don't use every day. Or said differently, when this stuff breaks, don't be in a hurry to replace it. If you can borrow it from your created family then do that, why don't you! While almost anything you want and need can be bought on credit, that doesn't mean you should do it. One less bill per month does add up.

In these days and times, there is only one appliance that you must absolutely have: and that is a computer.

Multiple televisions, radios, extra speakers... they are all things you don't really have to have...And even a computer you can work around, if you have a cell phone. Everything else you can get when you see fit.

COLLECTIVE WISDOM

#BUY WHEN YOU ARE READY

SO LET'S LOOK AT THE THINGS THAT YOU DON'T USE EVERY DAY INSIDE YOUR HOME:

    MIXER   VACUUM CLEANER
    TOASTER   WAFFLE IRON
    BROILER   HEDGE CLIPPERS
    DUTCH OVEN

... YOU GET THE POINT ...

GREGG ROBINSON

Net Worth Wipe Out

Regardless of what you think of the banks and whether or not they were complicit in the Great Recession, dwelling on it is useless folly.

Many of us who had savings saw significant portions of our net worth wiped out. Whether it was significant decreases in the value of our homes, major depreciation in our stock portfolios, 401K or similar plans or the value of other investments simply wiped out. For those of us that had little to no savings, we found ourselves even more stuck because people "with money" had no money to spend on discretionary items. Or in truth, it wasn't that they really didn't have any money, it's just that they weren't spending what they had. Everyone was waiting to see how the economic winds were going to blow.

So fast forward to 2016 when I started writing this book. Or now 2019 when I am finishing this book, we find that the stock market has returned to pre-2007 levels and in 2019 now well beyond, because it is grounded in market fundamentals and not real estate. This is touted by many investment advocates as proof that the market always returns. While I tend to agree with this perspective, we all know that, more so than some of our affluent friends and neighbors, that many of us didn't have the luxury of waiting it out. Lots of people took some serious hits. Many of us were devastated.

And what if you didn't have significant savings, and you were in finance or a real estate agent, or that waiter that got let go? The Great Recession was a pretty miserable period.

So where am I headed with this?

For way too many the economy hasn't really rebounded. The American Dream is being promoted as dead. Nobel laureates were on YouTube prognosticating the end of an era. The word socialism was casually being dropped in coffee shops near where I live. Discussions about sustainability abound.

Well my friends, the American Dream is not dead. It's just harder to achieve. And for those of you that live and work in geographic areas that are not growing, or are in industries that have plateaued, it's significantly harder for you.

So what's the purpose of this book and related podcasts?

To share concrete ideas on how to create surplus in your life. Small practical ideas that each and every one of us can do... if we want to.

→ And this book is geared for people that want to!

→ And there are lots of people just like you.

→ Frankly, there are tens of hundreds of people in this nation and truly around the world just like you.

This book is not for teaching you how to make a million dollars or to get rich in real estate...many books sell fantasy. **It irritates the hell out of me.** This book is about getting started: about building your foundation correctly. Get the first thousand in the bank. Get your first $5,000 in the bank. Make this the starter position.

Then you can read all the get rich books you want, LOL.

This book is about giving you encouragement - daily, next week, 3 months from now… whenever and where ever you pick it up. Just read a passage. Read a passage and know that somebody else is doing the same thing somewhere… around the corner, down the street, maybe even downstairs from you. Leave it in the kitchen. Let it get dirty. Ketchup stains on its pages would be the biggest compliment. Smudge marks on your phone are cool too.

And know that you are getting some solid advice on getting to a point where you are comfortable.

> So now, more than ever, the only person that can be counted on for your financial well-being is you and your family.

When you are at a point of comfort, you can make solid decisions on all aspects of your life. Who you love, what you care about, who you work for are so much easier if you know you are not facing financial ruin if you make a bad choice.

→ And frankly a good habit or two you pick up and use for the rest of your life will help you again if life deals you a bad hand.

Regardless of how you feel about this most recent financial debacle: many, perhaps most people were incredibly disappointed that few were prosecuted for any wrongdoing. For some of us disappointment is an understatement.

So now, more than ever, the only person that can be counted on for your financial well-being is you and your family.

The purpose of the book is to share with you many simple truths. To share and affirm ideas, stories and other lines of thought on how each and every one of you can create surplus in your life.

Surplus is simple: it's what you have left over at the end of the day, the week, or the month.

Yet in all its simplicity – it can be the hardest thing to do or the easiest thing to do. It's all in your attitude. It is also about creating connections that affirm you: that share your spirit.

And mostly, what we here at **Collective Wisdom** are about is affirming and re-affirming you – supporting you – in your decision to create surplus in your life.

Know that your are getting solid advice on getting to the point where you can be comfortable. For when you are at a point of comfort, your head is clear to make solid decisions on all aspects of your life.

OVERHEAD REDUCTION STRATEGIES

GREGG ROBINSON

Overhead Reduction Strategies

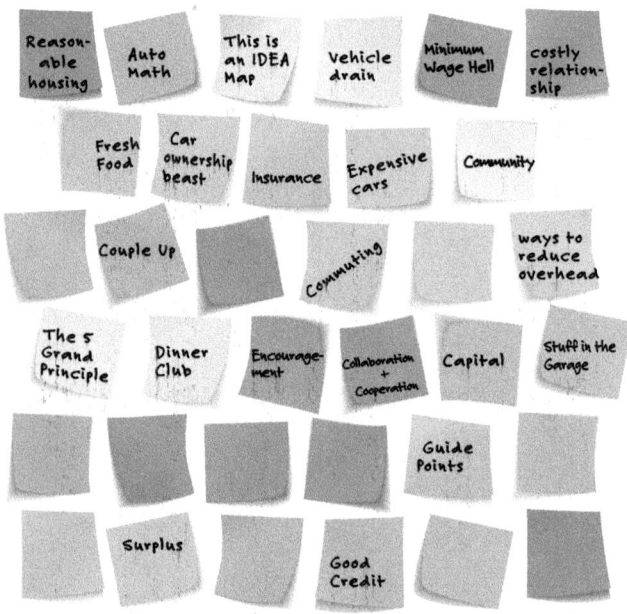

In the process of writing this book, my idea map was a series of sticky notes on one of my dining room walls. The idea below is a random thought that I thought deserved some mention. Not because it contributes significantly to the process of building or rebuilding. Yet after having numerous conversations with young people around the area, I wanted to dispel a particular notion. And that is, "wealthy" people don't buy used stuff... including clothes.

#GETTING IT TOGETHER

COLLECTIVE WISDOM

CLOTHING

Ever shop at Salvation Army? We are so wealthy as a nation now, you can go to a Salvation Army store anywhere in a reasonable driving distance from your home and get almost new clothes at a fraction of the price. Frankly, between Target and the online store of your choice, clothing is so cheap compared to twenty years ago I am surprised that I am even talking about it. Yet, aside from underwear, you can find almost everything you need at the SA. This includes towels, sheets, some furniture, kitchen appliances, etc. It might even be last season's stuff but do you think people really care? If you are out of work and hanging with the fashionistas, perhaps you need some new friends…at least temporarily.

If you really need to look good on that interview and you have to spring for something new, a properly fitted shirt and a new tie is your best bet. Go conservative and plain. This goes for women as well: plain shirt, pants/skirt depending on what region of the country you are in and the nature of the business and company you are trying to get to hire you. Unless it's a glam business: advertising, TV, radio, architecture, design, or other creative businesses that respect fashion forward or edgy people. Otherwise go basic.

Ever seen a designer consignment shoppe? That's affluent for used clothes.

Go get that paycheck: you can change your dress when those checks start rolling in and then you can be yourself more.

What I am talking about is that for many Americans under the age of 30, starting wages are too low in many large metropolitan areas. Yet solutions designed for large metropolitan areas are not always the best solutions for a nation as a whole. Realizing that activism has its limits - you can get out there and protest all you want - but I think there is another way to approach the subject. I would suggest just accept today's current reality and move on.

So let's roll.

What Am I Really Talking About Here?

COLLECTIVE WISDOM

There are only two ways to create surplus in your life: make more money than you spend OR spend less than you earn. That's it.

If you are an amateur student of history, you know that slavery was a means of creating massive amounts of monetary surplus for the upper classes of the time. Doesn't matter what century, what people, what region of the world – the details may vary but the concept is still the same. In the 21st century North America forced servitude has almost been eliminated. An environment exists that allows most people to be self-determining.

Self-determination with all its rights and responsibilities is a foundation block of a responsible democracy. Within this small literary work titled **Collective Wisdom** are ideas, some novel, some ever present yet written down too infrequently. **Collective Wisdom** is an expressed wish to provide those interested tools and friends to help you accomplish your goals.

#FOUNDATION BLOCK
#FRIENDS   #TOOLS
#DEMOCRACY

THE ASIAN PLAYBOOK

#SHARE
#SHARE SOMETHING

GREGG ROBINSON

The Asian Playbook

Let's take one from the Asian Playbook.

As immigrants to a foreign land, many new American families are huddling together in homes capable of accommodating multiple families yet designed as single family American homes. You may snub your nose at the eight cars in the driveway of your parents subdivision, but how quickly we forget. Or perhaps you are too young to know. This is no different than some of our predecessors in the 19th and early 20th centuries. Walk around any small town in America that's been around for at least a hundred years or so and tell me the history of that 3 story house now cut up into 8 apartments. I think you get my drift. It's a time honored tradition that many of us have forgot or simply forgotten to use as a wealth building tool.

So how do we update this?

Form your own families. Do you have a good size house or apartment with an extra bedroom or two? Rent it out at a competitive price to a friend or a new friend. Recent technologies have made this easy for you particularly if you live in a town or city that has a number of visitors.

Half the rent or mortgage payment is a significant boon to the bottom line for many people. Let's do some basic math. Let's say you rent the room for $500.00 per month with kitchen privileges, of course. That is a $6,000 dollar increase in your gross income! When is the last time you got a $6,000 raise!

COLLECTIVE WISDOM

Fresh Food Revisited

Passion for Carryout

It was not until I moved into the city, into an area with a complete mix of incomes, did I see people buy their dinners at the convenience store. Many times, these were young people whose mothers had sent them to the store to buy supper because she was working nights that week. (Yes, I know this family personally.) This particular liquor store had a fried chicken operation. Chicken was fresh, but for the life of me I couldn't tell where those green beans and mashed potatoes came from. My curious eyes were looking everywhere.

And by the way, that chicken dinner wasn't cheap.

Now before you jump all over me for being judgmental, and yes I am being seriously judgmental, let's talk about some fundamental differences.

Affluent women and men don't cook everyday — unless they like to, or see and appreciate the value of home cooked meals. High end grocery stores in affluent neighborhoods across the nation have prepared meals of varying quality ready and waiting for people that don't have time to cook, don't wish to cook, or flat out don't know how to cook. Generally speaking, foods prepared have average or above average ingredients, are prepared fresh daily, and are offered for sale at prices comparable to many restaurants. Grocery stores like this portion of their business because the mark-up is higher than the rest of the store operation.

That said, stores like this cater to the affluent or the wannabe affluent population. The chicken operation at the convenience store does not. They serve a deserving population, yet one that would be better served if it was profitable for a convenience store to offer a greater variety of fresh food. Unfortunately, it must not be otherwise they would all be doing it by now.

I am glad the chicken man is there: at least the chicken is real, not pre-packaged nonsense with only adequate nutritional value.

However, the real point is this: if you are working to create surplus in your life, eating food you cook yourself is more cost effective/money-wise than buying food out every day. You can always eat cheaper at home.

That is—if you can cook?

I have to tell you a story. I am going to change his name so that in case he reads my book... and I hope he does...he'll know that I know that he and I are the only ones that know I am talking about him. *Ahhhh...* I'm going to tell the story anyway.

COLLECTIVE WISDOM

THE BACKSTORY

My buddy, Brent, was the son of some big muckity muck in one of those congregations that is large enough to have its own national conference... know what I mean? Any way, Brent was 25 years old plus when we met. Both of us professional guys, we lived in the same apartment complex with a golf course and a few swimming pools in a well-healed Midwest city. I don't recall how we met. Yet, we crossed paths many a time and we became friends. Brent had a gift for gab that few surpassed.

As I began to know Brent, it became apparent that Brent ate out all of the time. Any time I was at the local watering hole, Brent was there having a drink or feeding his face. He was a fit guy so it appeared not to wear on him. Yet, I didn't discover that Brent couldn't cook until I picked him up one morning for a round of golf and he suggested we go to McDonald's. I asked him why. And he volunteered that he couldn't cook and that he needed something to eat before we rolled.

Honestly, I was taken aback. Actually I was shocked. I kept it under my lid that I was shocked that somebody who lives on his own couldn't cook so I played like it was no big deal. I grew up in a household of men who know how to cook. A man that doesn't know how to cook—get real.

But Brent didn't know how to cook, hadn't tried to learn how to cook, hadn't tried to teach himself to cook, and ate out every day – 24/7. This boy couldn't even boil an egg. Can you imagine how much he spent annually in restaurants? Even if you can't peel an onion, you can broil a steak, can't you?

That said, you know Brent was not on the path to create surplus in his life. He could recoup in other areas if he was determined to. Yet, to reduce expenses in this area is such an obvious thing to me. We all have our strengths.

AND WHEN YOU HAVE A PLAN

#DON'T BLOW IT ALL

#APPROPRIATE LEVEL OF RISK

#5 PERCENT OF SOMETHING IS 5% PLUS

GREGG ROBINSON

And When You Have A Plan

And when you have that great
idea you want to invest in...

ONLY USE 50% OF YOUR
WORKING CAPITAL.

Why? What if it fails?

Answer:

1. It is a lot easier to swallow a setback if you know that you have only lost half your money.

2. You still have funds that can be reinvested in the market.

3. It's easier to re-build something when you actually have something left.

It is as simple as this.

What if you only have $1000.00 left after it all comes crashing down?

That remaining money will earn a 5% return annually. At the end of the 12 months you will have at least $1050.00. On the other hand, five percent of zero is zero.

5% OF 0 IS ZERO

In summary, it's easier to swallow your temporary setback if you still have some cash left in your bank account.

THE MARKET

GREGG ROBINSON

The Market at this Stage of the Game

If you are starting out.

The stock market though attractive is not the spot for your collected savings just yet. Perhaps in a few years. The Big Exception is if your employer has offered you a 401K plan or the state or local government plan equivalent. Then take it. Put in as much as you can manage. If human resources at your workplace has a financial counselor on staff or an advisor they recommend and pay for, talk to them. Take note to see if your monthly deduction helps you drop a tax bracket. (Don't know what I am talking about? You will soon.) If it doesn't, do what is comfortable for your monthly budget, meaning your real expenses for the month.

There is no magic number for when to start investing in the stock market. Yet, one should have some savings first, well before making investments in other places. (Think: you've maintained at least $5,000 in the bank for a year or more now.)

A person should also have an interest in it – meaning have an active interest in the stock market. If you don't, there may be other places for you to invest your hard earned surplus. Maybe starting a business or investing in a family members business is something more to your liking. What is key is that it has to be something you have some first hand knowledge about. Educate yourself about an area of business that holds interest to you. YouTube is a great place to get an overview of almost anything you may be interested in. Yes, the Internet is really good for a few things.

Another really overlooked way to find out about almost anything is a book of fiction. A really good fiction writer strives to recreate reality to the best of their ability. Many of them are really good. Want to find out about something? Go to the library and discover it for free.

In truth, there are only 2 reasons we are mentioning the stock market to young people with limited business knowledge:

→ Interest rates are very low now and may remain low for quite some time.

→ The above fact makes bank savings accounts good for only some of your money.

Therefore, as you are building surplus, take some time and learn about businesses that interest you. You don't have to be an investment banker to know how to invest conservatively. Baseline knowledge about a company or an industry however helps.

GARAGE STUFF

So What About All That Stuff In The Garage

You Don't Have?

Let's say you are renting your first house. It has a decent sized lawn. Your new neighbor comes over and introduces himself. He sees that you don't have a lawnmower yet and offers to let you use his. Take him up on it. Swallow your pride for a second. Ask him if you can use if it for the season. And if he says yes, remember to always return it with a full tank of gas every time.

Save the $400.00, be a good neighbor and cut your grass once a week. And don't forget to return the favor twenty years from now when the new 25 year old kid moves in two doors down.

This works for other stuff too.

#Good Neighbor   #Be Kind

SO YOU ARE MAKING $62,500

So You are making $62,500 a year now. Very Cool.
TAKE A CHILL.
And don't get the most expensive car you can afford.

So You are Making $62,500

The Backstory

The most expensive car you can afford usually comes with the higher insurance rates. While this follows logically it's not always true, yet it's more often truer than not. Most of us like expensive things; expensive things cost more to maintain, cost more to insure because they cost more to fix, and more people want them than can afford them so they are more subject to the possibility of theft. Think about it.

Notice the behavior of some people with expensive cars. Some park near the rear of the parking lot and take up two parking spaces because they don't want someone to ding their paint jobs. Some people with expensive cars always valet or always use a pay parking lot. There's a hidden expense to an expensive car that you really shouldn't afford even if on paper it appears to be in your budget.

Be more moderate in your tastes - until you can really afford it.

Now if you really want to go deep, call your insurance agent and find out the insurance rates for the vehicle you want to buy before you buy it. The most popular car being stolen that year changes with the year and the geography. And it is near immediately reflected in the insurance rate for a particular vehicle. You, average citizen, can't predict it however, insurance companies quantify this type of data all of the time.

#CHILL #EXPENSIVE CARS

THE SUBJECT OF INSURANCE

OVERHEAD THAT YOU CANNOT AVOID

GREGG ROBINSON

The Subject of Insurance

Unfortunately, any state that has "no-fault" auto insurance mandates that every driver have insurance. Sometimes these states that mandate insurance for all drivers have a dysfunctional city or two with higher crime rates than the norm, and perhaps a correspondingly higher than normal car theft rate. Unfortunately, in-city residents often times have astronomically higher car insurance rates than suburbs immediately outside its borders. While this disparity is offensive to many, the purpose of the book is to emphasize that this is one area, insurance, where there are no work-arounds.

Well... no work-arounds that are in accordance with the law.

WOW. THERE IS NO WAY AROUND THIS ONE. IN SOME AREAS OF THE COUNTRY YOU SIMPLE CANNOT GET AROUND PAYING FOR INSURANCE REGARDLESS OF WHETHER CAN AFFORD IT OR NEED IT.

Here are some possible courses of actions:

→ **Get a car way below what you can afford per month.** It's not the tax, title and insurance at the time of purchase that will get you. That more expensive ride that you really like to look at and really like driving costs too much to insure as a percentage of your budget.

→ **If you get the more expensive ride, you also get the more expensive insurance. Period.**

→ **And by the way, you know you can call any experienced insurance agent and find out the most expensive car to insure in your area based on replacement parts and theft rates.** You can make it easy on your insurance agent and ask him/her to compare the rates on the top 3 vehicles you are considering purchasing. Just give him/her the make, model, year and engine size, and it's as simple as plugging in the numbers. If it's a used car, you may want to give him/her the mileage.

We have talked about whether it's time for a car yet in an earlier chapter. Let's be clear. The monthly car note payment, the monthly car insurance, and the gas, oil and other expenses, significantly knock up your operating expenses. **If you make less than $50,000 per year it is going to seriously impact your operating percentages.**

Renters or Contents Insurance

If you are just starting out, get the lowest content insurance that makes sense. I will suggest $5,000. If you are living in an apartment building and the stupid fool next door leaves the pasta boiling, runs out to get the tomato sauce she forgot, and her cat jumps on to the stove, accidentally pulling the dish towel over the burner, and it catches fire and so does the rest of the apartment... I know, real life is stranger than fiction... you can at least claim smoke or water damage for your contents if the local fire company has to hose down your place just to make sure they got all of the fire. Hmmm... maybe get ten thousand.

All jokes aside, this is the most reasonable insurance you will ever get. Fortunately for all of us, fire codes in this country are well designed, enforced on new construction, and have been proven effective over time.

Starting out or rebuilding your life? Get an adequate amount. And if you can't do that, get the smallest amount and then build it up as your budget allows.

Life Insurance

Well, if it's offered as a package at work and its cheap, get some. You never know what life has in store.

The stuff offered at work will most likely be a term policy. Keep in mind, this type of term life policy usually ends at the end of your employment with that company. Get it anyway if it's cheap and good. What's cheap? The monthly payment is so small you won't even notice it coming out of your check.

COLLECTIVE WISDOM

THE BACKSTORY

A $2,000 term life policy is not a good policy no matter how you slice it or dice it. I don't care how much it costs. You can't even get a good burial for 2 grand. I got a mailer from some bank or credit card company about a 2 grand term life insurance policy: I about puked. Are they crazy? Or do they really think I am that stupid?

Unfortunately, many of us at the lower end have credit card debt larger than that. So what is 2 grand going to do!?!

Bottom line is if you are going to get life insurance, make it a meaningful amount. As I stated earlier, it needs to be enough to pay off all your debts, pay for your burial, and deposit some cash in your friend's or relatives bank account so that they remember you fondly and not as a drain on their cash flow.

MORE BACK STORY ON INSURANCE

For a single person, life insurance is important if you have people that care about you OR you have people that you care about. In other words, if you got killed tomorrow in a car accident and you're leaving your Mom or Dad a car payment and a rental agreement, then get some life insurance: $10,000, $20,000 or $50,000. Get enough to settle your bills, pay for a decent funeral, and pass some money along to the people you care about or are dependent on you.

If you are married/coupled with children, it is even more important.

At this stage of the game, you just don't want to saddle people with your "stuff" just because you checked out earlier than expected.

As you start building up capital — meaning real stuff in your apartment or house that you can sell for cash and real money in your savings account... then you might want some real insurance.

No rush, but don't wait till your 60. I think whole life insurance makes sense for people building surpluses in their lives. Insurance reps have all kinds of products: get the one you understand.

GOOD CREDIT

GREGG ROBINSON

Good Credit

GOOD CREDIT AND A GOOD JOB

It's hard to say and a well-intentioned human resource person will never tell you, because they don't want to discourage you. On the flip, at some point during the interview process many potential employers will request your credit score from one of the three reporting services. You may ask yourself, what does it tell them?

Does it give a glimpse into your personality? Will a person who manages their own finances well be a person who manages people and situations well? Does it at least say that you honor your commitments?

So, what's up with this? Will a poor credit score keep me out of a job?

It probably won't keep you out of a low-paying job yet it might keep you out of a better paying job. That said, it is a good idea to keep an eye on it as you build or re-build your financial well-being.

#GOOD JOB   #GOOD CREDIT   #CREDIT SCORE

GOOD CREDIT AND A GOOD HOUSE

Will poor credit keep you out of a good house?

Well, my friends the Backstory tells it all. Good credit is most important in securing the principle wealth building block in contemporary society, *a home.*

#GOOD CREDIT   #CREDIT SCORE

COLLECTIVE WISDOM

THE BACKSTORY

Some Young People I Heard About

> This particular backstory also says something about the student loan situation in the United States. However that is not the purpose of our discussion here. Perhaps we will have a chance to talk about that in a related podcast.

Two young people I know of applied for a mortgage in a city not far away. Both happen to be doctors recently minted from their respective residency programs. They are married and are both employed physicians of a large medical concern. They figure it's time now to buy a house.

They found a lovely house in a great neighborhood befitting all the hard work they have put in to accomplish their professional goals. The home is very nice and the mortgage payment will fit well into their monthly budget. They apply for a mortgage expecting to skate right through considering their combined six figure incomes. However, they got a very rude surprise.

It turns out one of the spouses had not been paying on his undergraduate student loans. There were a couple of gap years between undergraduate and medical school for one of the spouses. Being a responsible person, he started paying on his loans after the six-month grace period. However, when he returned to school, he assumed that his loan balance would go into deferment until he finished medical school. He ignored the bills after having made his request for deferment thinking it was handled. Eventually the bills stopped coming. The spouse forgot about it.

Well, they didn't forget about him. Upon review of his credit rating after they so unfortunately, but appropriately got turned down, the couple discovers that one spouse has over six years of non-payment on this loan balance. Wow, crunch.

The couple decide on a smaller home to start. The credit-worthy spouse takes out the mortgage in one name only.

#KEEP AN EYE ON WHAT YOU HAVE BORROWED
#GOOD CREDIT

A DIFFERENT OVERHEAD REDUCTION STRATEGY

Take a moment to breathe.
Take a moment to meditate.
Take a moment to Pray.

GREGG ROBINSON

A Different Overhead Reduction Strategy

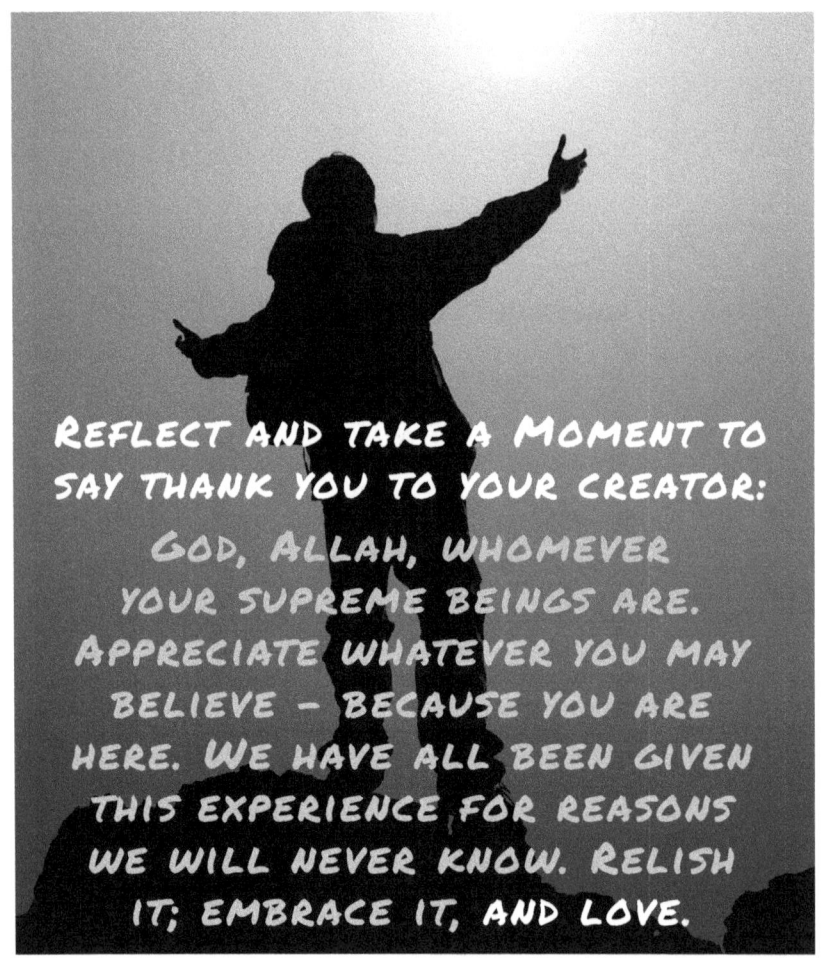

COLLECTIVE WISDOM

Final Thoughts

During the European expansion of the 19th century into the wooded nether lands of North America, settlers were advised to settle in groups. This was done for mutual support and to avoid the perils of isolation.

Fast forward to the first quarter of the 21st century. Like minded people, men and women with goals often times have a hard time finding each other.

What this book proposes is selective collectivism as a means of spiritual and financial enrichment. Help others as you help yourself.

The book, this set of ideas, provides constructs - to allow you to find other people like yourself who have goals, interests, or desire to do more with their lives.

Please use as you see fit.

GREGG ROBINSON

COLLECTIVE WISDOM

About the Author

The author had two children in his 40's and 50's and realized the expense of their likes: shopping, going out, great meals, cruising in cars and all the things that cost money. He made sure there was enough, managing through a divorce and maintaining savings to send one daughter off to college and prepping the younger since she was two. Accumulating tips throughout a half-century, Gregg shares his wisdom now written within.

The author subscribes to the axiom "once a Dad, always a Dad".

Follow Gregg Robinson on Facebook and Instagram.

Friends and followers stay tuned for **Collective Wisdom** on YouTube.

GREGG ROBINSON

COLLECTIVE WISDOM

Credits:

cover	84093042	©	Wavebreakmedia LTD
Illustration	120680104	©	Alexlmx
Illustration	120835043	©	Aquir
Illustration	120978458	©	Aquir
Illustration	148442446	©	Aquir
Illustration	89899694	©	Asmara, Andi
Illustration	104468361	©	Carlsen, Poul
Illustration	116783148	©	Decorwithme
Illustration	86667362	©	Dorney, Chris
Illustration	11533553	©	Frackowiak, Lukasz
Illustration	18782607	©	Georghiou, Christos
Illustration	2757713	©	Guan, Kheng
Illustration	144478808	©	Ivlicheva, Anastasia
Illustration	44631989	©	Katerinadav
Illustration	85493369	©	Levina, Alena
Illustration	27729673	©	Lhfgraphics
Illustration	153176659	©	Lineartestpilot
Illustration	153277157	©	Malkov, Evgeny
Illustration	22981686	©	Maximus256
Illustration	12234615	©	Micromann
Illustration	95240364	©	Nadiinko
Illustration	153622432	©	Naumov, Evgenii
Illustration	55172298	©	Perkov, Anatoliy
Illustration	115056227	©	PixMarket
Illustration	147007468	©	Sangkhamanee, Phongsak
Illustration	23315817	©	Skypixel
Illustration	123888562	©	Szczybylo, Artur
Illustration	123942703	©	Szczybylo, Artur
Illustration	9299073	©	Takai, John
Illustration	9584332	©	Takai, John
Illustration	19117823	©	Yaviki
Photo	120066391	©	An, Murat
Photo	149447275	©	Budkevics, Arturs
Photo	154701125	©	Fizkes
Photo	80071760	©	Guillem, Antonio
Photo	148872935	©	Kuprevich
Photo	104868330	©	Monkey Business Studio
Photo	36980496	©	Olson, Tyler
Photo	136371873	©	Scatena, Francesco
Photo	121883418	©	Szczybylo, Artur
Photo	13895504	©	Trekandshoot
Photo	32512713	©	Wavebreakmedia LTD
Photo	119358342	©	Welcomia
Photo	86496255	©	Wisconsinart
Photo	82320182	©	Wongsa, Jesada
Photo	147189509	©	Yalanskyi, Andrii
Photo	143361602	©	Yalanskyi, Andrii
Photo	139292928	©	Monthira Yodtiwong
Photo	161603604	©	Aleksandr Markin
Photo	46187351	©	Stnazkul
Photo	89124848	©	Antonio Guillem
Photo	140378468	©	Ernest Akayeu
Photo	128530109	©	Andrii Yalanskyi
Photo	132105359	©	Nuthawut Somsuk
Photo	159774549	©	Kritchai Chaibangyang
Photo	126514815	©	Thanasak Boonchoong
Photo	148843798	©	Katherinesizova
Photo	87568657	©	Grant Kinsey
Photo	67200220	©	Venusangel
Photo	78400985	©	Charlotte Lake
Photo	148517269	©	Wdnetagency
Photo	162328157	©	Mikabesfamilnaya

Photography & illustration manipulations by Laura Reynolds

www.ingramcontent.com/pod-product-compliance
Lightning Source LLC
Chambersburg PA
CBHW062051290426
44109CB00027B/2792